BYE BYE ANXIETY AND PANIC ATTACKS

Olga Gibbs

Raging Bear Publishing

FOREWORD

When I originally created "Anxiety Journal" in 2020, I wanted to create a sharp and practical tool, with which one can understand and, as a result, manage anxieties, and in some severe forms of anxiety – panic attacks.

Many "Anxiety Journals" on the market are filled with academic knowledge and language, with long lectures of an author on what the anxiety is, how it affects the body and mind. These books look more like encyclopaedia's entries into the disorder rather than a step by step guide on improving the condition.

Yet, anxiety is different in everyone, its manifestations differ in people, like with most of mental health issues, we might experience them differently.

This book is building and expanding on my earlier outlined proposed method of handling anxieties and repetitive, situational panic attacks, citing supporting evidence, which in turn, I hope, would confirm to readers that the road taken is the appropriate one. This edition is set to explain why we take this approach in managing an anxiety, why this practical and analytical approach is beneficial in your fight against the condition.

Yet, this book is going further than the "Anxiety Journal" did. It discusses avoidance and how it places anxiety out of the loop on new learnt experiences; this book later presents a range of exercises on improving the condition, such as exposure techniques, and then evaluates the post carried-out work episode vs the earlier episodes. This book provides a wide scope in techniques, research, and knowledge that CBT has collated in managing anxicty and panic attacks.

Hayes-Skelton illustrated in her research, worry and anxiety are usually maintained by a problematic and fused relationship with internal experiences, experiential **avoidance**, behavioural constriction and are reinforced through worry's function as a distraction from distressing topics. Therefore, effective treatments should modify these factors.

Strategies that cultivate mindfulness (a curious, non-judgmental awareness of the present moment, Kabat-Zinn, 2005), that promote de-centering (the process of seeing thoughts and feelings as objective events in the mind rather than personally identifying with them (Safran & Segal, 1990), that increase acceptance (the recognition that experiences will come and go and that judging or resisting them is not useful, which is in opposition to experiential avoidance (Hayes, Luoma, Bond, Masuda, & Lillis, 2006), and increase behavioural engagement should lead to changes in the symptoms of GAD (Generalised Anxiety Disorder) (Hayes-Skelton et al, "A Contemporary View of Applied Relaxation for Generalized Anxiety Disorder", Cognitive Behaviour Therapy Journal).

This book will be an invaluable practical tool in regards to your anxiety because it will look at the mentioned above factors and will provide exercises to modify them.

What will you find in this book? What can you expect from it?

First, we will collect data, recording occurring anxiety episodes or panic attacks in detail. This self-monitoring activity is an important first step, as by changing physiological responses to an episode, we can change, and eventually, break, the cycle of anxiety. As with the most of CBT-developed coping techniques, including the ones presented in this book, it requires understanding anxiety manifestations, situations of arousal, recognitions of the early signs of anxiety etc. in order to change the response cycle.

Then, we will analyse the collected data, and that is why we need a generous amount of data to work with. This data is invaluable in understanding the anxiety or causes for panic attacks: in understanding anxiety's manifestations – mental and physical – the effect it has on us and on our lives, our body and mind, noting situations in which anxiety or panic attacks occur, under which stimuli. Using that data, later we will develop personalised avoidance hierarchy, anxiety hierarchy and then, coping mechanisms.

During the next step in analysing the data, we will look for patterns: patterns in our responses and patterns in external and internal stimuli – "what", "when" and "why" during each episode: what we were doing; where we were etc. It is important to gather the personalised data, so later we can analyse it, looking for patterns, as more often than not, anxiety or panic episodes are tend to occur under the same stimuli, time and time again. This type of analysis could also be beneficial in other forms of personal and inter-personal therapy, although it is rarely practiced with the same intensity and focus, as when dealing with anxiety.

At the next step on our journey towards recovery, we'll evaluate triggers. As an integral part of the analysis, we will collate the personal list of triggers, whilst looking back at the recorded data. We will arrange hen these triggers from the most tolerable to the least tolerable, indicating situations in which anxiety occurred.

Then, we will find avoidance behaviour patterns in ourselves and construct a personal avoidance hierarchy. Just as with the triggers, we need to understand the situations, which we find too difficult to handle or confront, situation which we tend to avoid, and for that we too need the gathered data.

We need to work on eliminating vigilance-avoidance pattern of behaviours in ourselves, as proven by research of Vassiopoulos, "a vigilance-avoidance pattern of processes for threat-relevant cues is the reason for the maintenance of social anxiety" ("Social Anxiety and the Vigilance-Avoidance Pattern of Attentional Processing", Behavioural and Cognitive Psychotherapy, 2005). Simply speaking: we don't allow ourselves to learn that sometimes identical situations might have different outcome or that with a bit of work, we can turn and change the outcome of a potentially stressful situation. Our bias learning is set to the notion that "Situation X = danger". We're allowing fear of the past learnings dominate an outcome of potentially different situation, as a result, narrowing our real-life exposure and cycles, limiting our lives, the joy of exploration, curiosity and overall life enjoyment.

At the next stage, we will try to approach the identified anxious situations from a different angle, with a view to diminish the stress response in short-term. I would like to emphasise the word "short-term", as we're not here to develop a long-term avoidance pattern, but, by modifying the level of stress from stimuli, get slowly accustomed to the real-life stress factors, like getting used to cold water.

Then, as we progress with the proposed change in the mind set, this book will progress with identified triggers and steps that one could take towards the controlled exposure, in order to improve severity of panic attacks, lessen the triggers and anxiety episodes.

And finally, the book will culminate with evaluation of the results. In the specially designed tables, with specially developed prompts, we will then analyse side by side the earlier triggers, situational avoidance patterns (and change in their hierarchy), severity of panic attacks etc, after the proposed work of data gathering and exposure exercises has been concluded.

The final look into "what worked and what haven't" should demonstrate to us which techniques in managing anxiety and panic attacks we had found most useful, which had delivered the better results, etc. This should give us insight into what works for us and what doesn't, as I say later, when we explore our anxiety: Anxieties are not identical in two people: we experience them differently, we have different triggers, different soothing mechanisms; our reactions to the world, negative and positive, are as unique as we're, and understanding them is the crucial first step in developing managing strategies.

PART 1
INTRODUCTION

INTRODUCTION

Anxiety refers to multiple mental and physiological phenomena, including a person's conscious state of worry over a future unwanted event, or fear of an actual situation (Evans et al, "Treating and preventing adolescent mental health disorders", Oxford Medicine). Some researchers define anxiety simply as "inability to regulate emotions", whilst others tie anxiety with an error-related brain activity.

But irrespective of the definition, all health experts agree that understanding anxieties is the first step in managing them.

Anxiety can be a crippling mental health issue to live with. It can affect our day-to-day living, our enjoyment of life, and can have negative effect on professional life, self-esteem, personal life, relationships and social interaction.

Panic is the most severe form of anxiety. Panic disorder is an anxiety disorder where you regularly have sudden attacks of panic or fear. During a panic attack you get a rush of intense mental and physical symptoms, at it's the most crippling and heightened form of anxiety disorder.

CBT (Cognitive Behavioural Therapy) has been deemed the most successful in delivering the best results in anxiety management. CBT focuses on how our thoughts, beliefs and attitudes affect our feelings and subsequent behaviour. CBT aims to stop negative thoughts cycles by breaking them down and making problems more manageable. CBT helps to change the negative thought pattern, to analyse anxieties and its triggers by finding thought or situational patterns.

Usually, in CBT you will be working with a therapist to identify those patterns of thought and behaviour, but ultimately, once you have identified those thoughts and behaviours, you can challenge them, in turn changing the way you feel in certain situations, thus managing and changing your behavioural response to those situations in future.

As much as all types of journaling, including gratitude journaling, have been found to be very beneficial in managing anxieties, this journal has been developed especially with anxieties management in mind.

This book holds two sets of anxiety developed questionnaires, with questions designed to understand your, personal anxieties, conditions and situations, during which they occurred, then analysing the outcome of each episode. The questionnaire for each anxiety episode is then supported by a gratitude prompt, to end the reliving of an anxious episode, and its evaluation, on a positive note.

By analysing anxieties and its triggers, this book will provide you with deeper understanding of your mental health condition, discovering repetitions in triggers, conditions and situations, thus future-proofing your anxiety management by changing your behavioural response to a potentially anxious situation.

WHY ANXIETY WORKBOOK?

Understanding anxiety is the first step in managing it. In knowing its erratic nature, we can obtain a better sense of triggering situations and how our anxiety operates. Left unchecked, anxiety can lead to stress and rumination, as some of the roots of your anxiety can be minimized through focused examination.

This book will assist you in examining and shifting thoughts from anxious and ruminative to empowered and action-oriented. This book, with self-analysing prompts, will help you to write yourself out of stress and anxiety, by better understanding your anxiety and its triggers, while providing management and relief techniques.

The data gathering section of this book is developed on the "Action-Focused Journaling" technique. It will assist you in putting your worries and concerns to paper, examining and investigating them, while finding a pattern, then reflecting, and finally "exiting smart": armed with knowledge, with coping strategies and better understanding of yourself.

HOW TO RECORD DATA

The evidence-gathering section of this book is designed to provide you with a space to record, evaluate and understand your anxieties. It holds forty pages of anxiety records, forty pages of gratitude prompts – both as tools for confronting and understanding your anxiety.

There are two ways to record your anxieties: a log with prompt questions and a log, arranged as a table, and there are twenty of each. Please try both, later utilising a preferred format of recording the data.

Carry this book with you, record in it every time you experience anxiety. Write freely and honestly. Don't be afraid to sound "silly" or "overreacting" – this is your private space. This data will be invaluable in developing coping mechanisms and evaluating triggers later, so the honesty is the key!

A SIDE NOTE: TREATMENT OF ANXIETY WITH CBT:

1. Psych-education – understanding what anxiety is and how it affects you.
2. Challenging negative thoughts – acknowledgement of thoughts contributing to anxiety, whilst putting fears into perspective.
3. Exposure therapy – controlled or measured exposure to the identified source of anxiety.
4. Relaxation skills – personal techniques that initiating calming response.

When one would work with a therapist on eliminating, or at least, elevating, anxieties' symptoms, one would be taken down the above, simplified, 4-steps path in order to improve the condition.

Four steps, four skills that one would be asked to master in order to become anxiety-free: understanding, acknowledging, exposure and relaxation – all of which we will cover in this book.

PART 2
ANXIETY: IT'S PERSONAL

MY ANXIETY AND ME

It is important to understand your anxiety. Many anxiety books inform you on what you might experience when anxiety or panic attacks come. They tell you that you might feel shortage of breath or rapid breathing, have a feeling of constriction in your chest, sweaty palms etc. But there are examples, in psychology and psychiatry literature, of sufferers who reported hot flashes during their anxiety episodes, a pulsating inside their head, even utilising skin-pulling or a self-mutilating act of any other kind, especially if their anxiety manifests on the backdrop of other underlining mental health conditions (Fromm-Reichmann, "Psychotherapy of schizophrenia", American Journal of Psychiatry).

And before we progress further, in order to improve the condition, you need to understand your anxiety.

I invite you to take a moment and meet it, acknowledge it and record effects it has on your body and mind.

Using free-writing and drawing techniques, explore your memories of your past anxiety episode, thus exploring and investigating your, personal anxiety.

Before you would be in a position to manage your anxiety and its manifestations effectively, and above all sustainably, you need to understand that everyone experiences anxiety or panic episodes differently, and therefore, would need to record your anxiety manifestations. Not only through this you'll understand your anxiety better, which will be invaluable in successful management of the condition and its episodes, but it will provide you with the data of early warning signs of impending anxiety episodes.

Equipped with knowledge of your anxiety, and later, with management techniques that you'd develop towards the end of this book, you will be able to manage your response to the triggers, which you will record in this journal too.

This is not an empty exercise of aimlessly collecting the data. These two exercises are the first two steps towards gathering the invaluable data, which later would be utilised in creating coping mechanisms and techniques. This data is the first step towards understanding your anxiety: its triggers (situational, social or internal) and its manifestations. We are looking for a pattern, and this is the first step in establishing one.

MY ANXIETY LOOKS LIKE THIS:

This space is for you to look deeper into your mind and release the grip on your self-conciseness. Let your body and mind take over. Feel free to doodle, use different colours, scribble. There is no wrong or right way to explore your anxiety.

WHEN ANXIETY COMES, IT FEELS LIKE THIS:

This is the space for your "free writing" exercise to investigate what effect anxiety has on your body, so that you can work on controlling your body, thus controlling anxiety.

50 THINGS THAT MAKE ME ANXIOUS OR STRESSED:

There's no rush to write these all at once. Make this list during your period of working through this book. Understanding anxiety triggers is one of the most important steps in managing anxiety.

50 THINGS THAT MAKE ME HAPPY:

You don't have to complete this list in one go. Take your time. Reflect. Understanding your happy spaces will later provide you with coping mechanisms.

MEDITATION

Relaxation skills are important in managing anxiety, and the meditation has been found particularly effective in managing this mental health condition.

A review of the impact of mindfulness-based stress reduction (MBSR) programme on the symptoms of anxiety had demonstrated that a mindfulness meditation training program has effectively reduced symptoms of anxiety and panic, and that it can help maintain these reductions in patients with generalized anxiety disorder, panic disorder, or panic disorder with agoraphobia (Kabat-Zinn et al, "Effectiveness of a meditation-based stress reduction program in the treatment of anxiety disorders", The American Journal of Psychiatry).

Armed with the knowledge of beneficial effects of meditation on anxiety, you're invited to practice a meditation technique of your choosing and record it in the provided table, on the next page. As well as being asked to meditate, there you will be asked to record the length of your meditation, whilst scoring the intensity of your anxiety at the beginning and the end of the meditation session.

Of course, meditation is not the only tactic that could be used to reduce the stress or anxiety. It is important to develop those personal, and sustainable, relaxation skills and techniques, not only to aid post-episode recovery, to be used later once the exposure therapy is initiated, but to implement them at the first signs of anxiety or a panic attack.

Meditation is the key!

Anxiety is a cognitive state connected to the inability to regulate emotions. But research shows that consistent meditation practice reprograms neural pathways in the brain, and therefore, improves our ability to regulate emotions.

Use the table below to rate your anxiety level from 1 to 10 (1 is calm and 10 is very anxious) before and after meditation, noting the length of meditation. Find your favourite meditation technique, or just sit in a quiet room, listening to your own heartbeat and being in the moment.

Should you have severe anxiety, or if you've been diagnosed with anxiety disorder, speak to your healthcare professional to discuss your options and figure out how to make meditation a component of your overall treatment program.

Date	How long did you meditate?	How did you feel before meditation?	How did you feel after meditation?

ANXIETY AND GRATITUDE: WHY DO WE NEED TO GIVE GRATITUDE?

Professor of Psychology A. Wood had described dispositional gratitude as an integral part of a wider life orientation towards noticing and appreciating the positive aspects in one's life and the world. He said that a life orientation towards the positive is incompatible with the "negative triad" of beliefs about self, world and future, which is typical of the depressive mind-set (Wood et al, "Gratitude and well-being: A review and theoretical integration", Clinical Psychology Review).

Several empirical studies have established links between gratitude and lower levels of psychopathological symptoms, in particular depression and anxiety. Gratitude, as an "other-oriented" process, has been found to promote pro-social behaviour, improving relationships with others. Gratitude was also associated with the improved "relationship with the self," in the form of a more positive and compassionate way of treating ourselves when things go wrong in life, which explains why grateful people are also less depressed and anxious.

Recent findings suggest that the grateful disposition is connected to a higher secretion of oxytocin, a neuropeptide that has been shown to lead to social approach-related motivation and behaviour, which in turn was enhancing self-attribution of positive adjectives, thus improving the representation of self, improving positive self-perceptions and openness to experiences (Algoe & Way, "Evidence for a role of the oxytocin system, indexed by genetic variation in CD38, in the social bonding effects of expressed gratitude", Social Cognitive and Affective Neuroscience).

Through the empirical research, Dr Petrocchi had demonstrated that the grateful disposition represents a protective factor against depression and anxiety, partly because it is connected to a lower level of feelings of inadequacy and self-denigration, but also lowers self-hate and self-repugnance, which represent more severe forms of self-criticism.

Dr Petrocchi had found that grateful people experience less anxiety mostly because they are able to encourage and be compassionate and reassuring toward themselves when things go wrong in life. Moreover, grateful people may possess a worldview that is more focused on the appreciation of the good things in life, including personal qualities, skills, and resources ("The impact of gratitude on depression and anxiety: the mediating role of criticizing, attacking, and reassuring the self", Self and Identity, Vol 15, 2016).

Therefore, it has been proven that a grateful mind-set promotes positive changes in mental health in long-term, and reduces depression and anxiety.

Backed with such unequivocal evidence, you can see why gratitude is so important in our lives, and why do we need to practice it.

So, in order to lessen negative effects of the emotional response to the anxiety episode on our self-image, after each recorded episode, we will take a moment and look for a few things in our lives that we could be grateful for, irrelevant how small they might seem to our mind.

We need to do it in order to rebuild our positive self-image, our self-belief and the view of ourselves after an anxiety episode.

The moments of happiness

The long-term benefits of concentrating on positivity are well documented; therefore, we are going to look for rays of sunshine in otherwise dark stormy skies. We need to learn to look for positivity in otherwise ordinary or challenging days. So, note something positive in here.

Did someone say something nice to you, give you a compliment or say that they love you? Maybe someone picked up a glove that you dropped or simply smiled at you? No matter how small, note these little rays of sunshine here.

Date	What positive moment had happened?	Had you noticed it at that time?	Would you spot a similar positive moment in the future?

PART 3
DATA COLLECTION

TRIGGERS: WHY DO WE NEED TO KNOW AND ANALYSE THEM?

Why knowing and understanding triggers is the only, and sustainable, way forward in managing anxieties?

As we work with anxiety, first and foremost, we need to identify specific triggers that prompt our anxiety episodes. Through understanding and recording triggers not only we would be able to note our emotions (fear and worry) during a particular situation, but we'd be able to note the subsequent avoidance strategies we use – the strategies that we implement in a bid to avoid unpleasant, uncomfortable situations.

The ostrich's head in the sand is the best analogy to the avoidance strategies. Although the ostrich can't see risks or dangers around him, his "head in the sand" *avoidance* strategy acts as a pacifier to his fears, the danger still remains around him – it didn't go anywhere, and his body is still exposed to predators.

Of course, sometimes, there are barriers in identifying triggers. Sometimes, sufferers are too reluctant to disclose them, have developed such complex avoidance patterns that the trigger are unclear to them, or they can become so overwhelmed by the emotion that they cannot recognize a specific trigger.

There is plenty of evidence indicating that cognitive–behavioural therapy (CBT) and, specifically, measured and controlled exposure, in its various forms, is the most effective method in treating anxiety disorders. With the evidential base on the triggers' pattern, social or situational, anxious emotions, and avoidance behaviour, one can begin to map out approaches to exposure therapy. The interventions utilized in CBT share clear similarities to exposure with response prevention – a type of exposure therapy commonly used with OCD.

So let's proceed with gathering the data (below).

ANXIETY RECORDS

DATE:

Why am I worried today?

How severe is my anxiety today? (Mark it from 1 to 10, where 1 is being calm and 10 is being very anxious)

What am I thinking?

What's the proof that it will happen?

What's the proof that it won't happen?

So what if it happens?

How can I deal with it?

What can I say and do to help me to get through this?

OUTCOME

Please record if your fears came true. What was the outcome of that anxiety episode? Were you right to worry? Be honest.

LET'S GIVE GRATITUDE!

We've discuss the benefits of gratitude-giving above and of the importance of ending an episode on a positive note.

So, without a further ado, list three things that you've enjoyed today or which made you happy, no matter how small. We need to see that even in anxiety-filled days we have something to be thankful for.

1.

2.

3.

ANXIETY RECORDS

DATE:

Why am I worried today?

How severe is my anxiety today? (Mark it from 1 to 10, where 1 is being calm and 10 is being very anxious)

What am I thinking?

What's the proof that it will happen?

What's the proof that it won't happen?

So what if it happens?

How can I deal with it?

What can I say and do to help me get through this?

OUTCOME

Please record if your fears came true. What was the outcome of that anxiety episode? Were you right to worry? Be honest.

LET'S GIVE GRATITUDE!

List three things that you've enjoyed today or which made you happy, no matter how small. We need to see that even in anxiety-filled days we have something to be thankful for.

1.

2.

3.

ANXIETY RECORDS

DATE:

Why am I worried today?

How severe is my anxiety today? (Mark it from 1 to 10, where 1 is being calm and 10 is being very anxious)

What am I thinking?

What's the proof that it will happen?

What's the proof that it won't happen?

So what if it happens?

How can I deal with it?

What can I say and do to help me get through this?

OUTCOME

Please record if your fears came true. What was the outcome of that anxiety episode? Were you right to worry? Be honest.

LET'S GIVE GRATITUDE!

List three things that you've enjoyed today or which made you happy, no matter how small. We need to see that even in anxiety-filled days we have something to be thankful for.

1.

2.

3.

ANXIETY RECORDS

DATE:

Why am I worried today?

How severe is my anxiety today? (Mark it from 1 to 10, where 1 is being calm and 10 is being very anxious)

What am I thinking?

What's the proof that it will happen?

What's the proof that it won't happen?

So what if it happens?

How can I deal with it?

What can I say and do to help me get through this?

OUTCOME

Please record if your fears came true. What was the outcome of that anxiety episode? Were you right to worry? Be honest.

LET'S GIVE GRATITUDE!

List three things that you've enjoyed today or which made you happy, no matter how small. We need to see that even in anxiety-filled days we have something to be thankful for.

1.

2.

3.

ANXIETY RECORDS

DATE:

Why am I worried today?

How severe is my anxiety today? (Mark it from 1 to 10, where 1 is being calm and 10 is being very anxious)

What am I thinking?

What's the proof that it will happen?

What's the proof that it won't happen?

So what if it happens?

How can I deal with it?

What can I say and do to help me get through this?

OUTCOME

Please record if your fears came true. What was the outcome of that anxiety episode? Were you right to worry? Be honest.

LET'S GIVE GRATITUDE!

List three things that you've enjoyed today or which made you happy, no matter how small. We need to see that even in anxiety-filled days we have something to be thankful for.

1.

2.

3.

ANXIETY RECORDS

DATE:

Why am I worried today?

How severe is my anxiety today? (Mark it from 1 to 10, where 1 is being calm and 10 is being very anxious)

What am I thinking?

What's the proof that it will happen?

What's the proof that it won't happen?

So what if it happens?

How can I deal with it?

What can I say and do to help me get through this?

OUTCOME

Please record if your fears came true. What was the outcome of that anxiety episode? Were you right to worry? Be honest.

LET'S GIVE GRATITUDE!

List three things that you've enjoyed today or which made you happy, no matter how small. We need to see that even in anxiety-filled days we have something to be thankful for.

1.

2.

3.

ANXIETY RECORDS

DATE:

Why am I worried today?

How severe is my anxiety today? (Mark it from 1 to 10, where 1 is being calm and 10 is being very anxious)

What am I thinking?

What's the proof that it will happen?

What's the proof that it won't happen?

So what if it happens?

How can I deal with it?

What can I say and do to help me get through this?

OUTCOME

Please record if your fears came true. What was the outcome of that anxiety episode? Were you right to worry? Be honest.

LET'S GIVE GRATITUDE!

List three things that you've enjoyed today or which made you happy, no matter how small. We need to see that even in anxiety-filled days we have something to be thankful for.

1.

2.

3.

ANXIETY RECORDS

DATE:

Why am I worried today?

How severe is my anxiety today? (Mark it from 1 to 10, where 1 is being calm and 10 is being very anxious)

What am I thinking?

What's the proof that it will happen?

What's the proof that it won't happen?

So what if it happens?

How can I deal with it?

What can I say and do to help me to get through this?

OUTCOME

Please record if your fears came true. What was the outcome of that anxiety episode? Were you right to worry? Be honest.

LET'S GIVE GRATITUDE!

List three things that you've enjoyed today or which made you happy, no matter how small. We need to see that even in anxiety-filled days we have something to be thankful for.

1.

2.

3.

ANXIETY RECORDS

DATE:

Why am I worried today?

How severe is my anxiety today? (Mark it from 1 to 10, where 1 is being calm and 10 is being very anxious)

What am I thinking?

What's the proof that it will happen?

What's the proof that it won't happen?

So what if it happens?

How can I deal with it?

What can I say and do to help me get through this?

OUTCOME

Please record if your fears came true. What was the outcome of that anxiety episode? Were you right to worry? Be honest.

LET'S GIVE GRATITUDE!

List three things that you've enjoyed today or which made you happy, no matter how small. We need to see that even in anxiety-filled days we have something to be thankful for.

1.

2.

3.

ANXIETY RECORDS

DATE:

Why am I worried today?

How severe is my anxiety today? (Mark it from 1 to 10, where 1 is being calm and 10 is being very anxious)

What am I thinking?

What's the proof that it will happen?

What's the proof that it won't happen?

So what if it happens?

How can I deal with it?

What can I say and do to help me get through this?

OUTCOME

Please record if your fears came true. What was the outcome of that anxiety episode? Were you right to worry? Be honest.

LET'S GIVE GRATITUDE!

List three things that you've enjoyed today or which made you happy, no matter how small. We need to see that even in anxiety-filled days we have something to be thankful for.

1.

2.

3.

TEN ANXIETY EPISODES RECORDED, THEN BALANCED WITH THE "TEN MOMENTS OF GRATITUDE": NOW WHAT?

"Recognizing one's own emotions is an essential skill from which other skills necessary for both therapy and emotional self-control stem."

Jan Prasko, Professor, MD in Psychiatry.

Reflection is an essential component of self-growth. Osterman describes it as the essential part of leaning, because it involves making sense of, or extracting meaning from, experience. Specifically, he states that "without reflection, theories of action are not revised and, until new concepts, ideas or theories of action begin to influence behaviour, learning will not occur" (Osterman, "Reflective practice: A new agenda for education", Education and Urban Society). So put it simpler, our life won't begin to change for the better until we recognise the need for change, then proceeding to change our behaviour, and the way we respond to the world. For us to gain genuine knowledge from an experience, we must be willing to be involved in the experience and be able to reflect on the experience. Basically, we are learning, and improving, by looking back and reflecting.

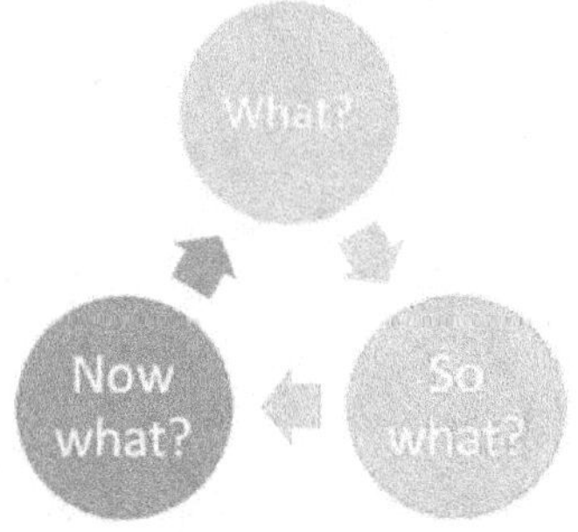

Rolfe et al.'s (2001) reflective model.

Reflective practice is not always comfortable or pleasant experience; however through this, we not only grow, but we obtain control over our mind and body through understanding the reasoning behind our behaviour, as reflective practice is essential in developing behavioural and cognitive flexibility.

With the importance of reflective practice on learning and developing new habits, I'd like to introduce, and reiterate, one more rule to the reflective practice when it comes to anxiety: kindness to yourself.

Although reflective practice requires critical thinking, we need to be measured in self-reflection, and realise that self-reflection and self-criticism is not the same thing. We need to reflect on our failings and shortcomings with kindness, acceptance and forgiveness. This is a journey, and you're only taking a few first steps down this long road. It might be a while before you'll see improvements, it might be sooner, but irrelevant of the timeframe in which you will achieve your goal, you need to be kind and patient to yourself throughout this experience.

With that knowledge at hand, we pause the data gathering and on the next page reflect on the last ten, recorded episodes.

The reflection corner

Please use this page to reflect on the last ten anxiety episodes.

Using free writing, look back, evaluate them, noting your "low points" (when you were stressed the most), noting situational, social or internal conditions surrounding the episodes. If you can, try to narrow down to what had prompted the episode.

Once you have concluded your anxiety reflection, try to recall a few happy moments within the same timeframe, if you can.

DATA COLLECTION: ANOTHER TEN EPISODES

ANXIETY RECORDS

DATE:

Why am I worried today?

How severe is my anxiety today? (Mark it from 1 to 10, where 1 is being calm and 10 is being very anxious)

What am I thinking?

What's the proof that it will happen?

What's the proof that it won't happen?

So what if it happens?

How can I deal with it?

What can I say and do to help me to get through this?

OUTCOME

Please record if your fears came true. What was the outcome of that anxiety episode? Were you right to worry? Be honest.

LET'S GIVE GRATITUDE!

List three things that you've enjoyed today or which made you happy, no matter how small. We need to see that even in anxiety-filled days we have something to be thankful for.

1.

2.

3.

ANXIETY RECORDS

DATE:

Why am I worried today?

How severe is my anxiety today? (Mark it from 1 to 10, where 1 is being calm and 10 is being very anxious)

What am I thinking?

What's the proof that it will happen?

What's the proof that it won't happen?

So what if it happens?

How can I deal with it?

What can I say and do to help me get through this?

OUTCOME

Please record if your fears came true. What was the outcome of that anxiety episode? Were you right to worry? Be honest.

LET'S GIVE GRATITUDE!

List three things that you've enjoyed today or which made you happy, no matter how small. We need to see that even in anxiety-filled days we have something to be thankful for.

1.

2.

3.

ANXIETY RECORDS

DATE:

Why am I worried today?

How severe is my anxiety today? (Mark it from 1 to 10, where 1 is being calm and 10 is being very anxious)

What am I thinking?

What's the proof that it will happen?

What's the proof that it won't happen?

So what if it happens?

How can I deal with it?

What can I say and do to help me get through this?

OUTCOME

Please record if your fears came true. What was the outcome of that anxiety episode? Were you right to worry? Be honest.

LET'S GIVE GRATITUDE!

List three things that you've enjoyed today or which made you happy, no matter how small. We need to see that even in anxiety-filled days we have something to be thankful for.

1.

2.

3.

ANXIETY RECORDS

DATE:

Why am I worried today?

How severe is my anxiety today? (Mark it from 1 to 10, where 1 is being calm and 10 is being very anxious)

What am I thinking?

What's the proof that it will happen?

What's the proof that it won't happen?

So what if it happens?

How can I deal with it?

What can I say and do to help me get through this?

OUTCOME

Please record if your fears came true. What was the outcome of that anxiety episode? Were you right to worry? Be honest.

LET'S GIVE GRATITUDE!

List three things that you've enjoyed today or which made you happy, no matter how small. We need to see that even in anxiety-filled days we have something to be thankful for.

1.

2.

3.

ANXIETY RECORDS

DATE:

Why am I worried today?

How severe is my anxiety today? (Mark it from 1 to 10, where 1 is being calm and 10 is being very anxious)

What am I thinking?

What's the proof that it will happen?

What's the proof that it won't happen?

So what if it happens?

How can I deal with it?

What can I say and do to help me get through this?

OUTCOME

Please record if your fears came true. What was the outcome of that anxiety episode? Were you right to worry? Be honest.

LET'S GIVE GRATITUDE!

List three things that you've enjoyed today or which made you happy, no matter how small. We need to see that even in anxiety-filled days we have something to be thankful for.

1.

2.

3.

ANXIETY RECORDS

DATE:

Why am I worried today?

How severe is my anxiety today? (Mark it from 1 to 10, where 1 is being calm and 10 is being very anxious)

What am I thinking?

What's the proof that it will happen?

What's the proof that it won't happen?

So what if it happens?

How can I deal with it?

What can I say and do to help me get through this?

OUTCOME

Please record if your fears came true. What was the outcome of that anxiety episode? Were you right to worry? Be honest.

LET'S GIVE GRATITUDE!

List three things that you've enjoyed today or which made you happy, no matter how small. We need to see that even in anxiety-filled days we have something to be thankful for.

1.

2.

3.

ANXIETY RECORDS

DATE:

Why am I worried today?

How severe is my anxiety today? (Mark it from 1 to 10, where 1 is being calm and 10 is being very anxious)

What am I thinking?

What's the proof that it will happen?

What's the proof that it won't happen?

So what if it happens?

How can I deal with it?

What can I say and do to help me to get through this?

OUTCOME

Please record if your fears came true. What was the outcome of that anxiety episode? Were you right to worry? Be honest.

LET'S GIVE GRATITUDE!

List three things that you've enjoyed today or which made you happy, no matter how small. We need to see that even in anxiety-filled days we have something to be thankful for.

1.

2.

3.

ANXIETY RECORDS

DATE:

Why am I worried today?

How severe is my anxiety today? (Mark it from 1 to 10, where 1 is being calm and 10 is being very anxious)

What am I thinking?

What's the proof that it will happen?

What's the proof that it won't happen?

So what if it happens?

How can I deal with it?

What can I say and do to help me get through this?

OUTCOME

Please record if your fears came true. What was the outcome of that anxiety episode? Were you right to worry? Be honest.

LET'S GIVE GRATITUDE!

List three things that you've enjoyed today or which made you happy, no matter how small. We need to see that even in anxiety-filled days we have something to be thankful for.

1.

2.

3.

ANXIETY RECORDS

DATE:

Why am I worried today?

How severe is my anxiety today? (Mark it from 1 to 10, where 1 is being calm and 10 is being very anxious)

What am I thinking?

What's the proof that it will happen?

What's the proof that it won't happen?

So what if it happens?

How can I deal with it?

What can I say and do to help me get through this?

OUTCOME

Please record if your fears came true. What was the outcome of that anxiety episode? Were you right to worry? Be honest.

LET'S GIVE GRATITUDE!

List three things that you've enjoyed today or which made you happy, no matter how small. We need to see that even in anxiety-filled days we have something to be thankful for.

1.

2.

3.

ANXIETY RECORDS

DATE:

Why am I worried today?

How severe is my anxiety today? (Mark it from 1 to 10, where 1 is being calm and 10 is being very anxious)

What am I thinking?

What's the proof that it will happen?

What's the proof that it won't happen?

So what if it happens?

How can I deal with it?

What can I say and do to help me get through this?

OUTCOME

Please record if your fears came true. What was the outcome of that anxiety episode? Were you right to worry? Be honest.

LET'S GIVE GRATITUDE!

List three things that you've enjoyed today or which made you happy, no matter how small. We need to see that even in the anxiety-filled days we have something to be thankful for.

1.

2.

3.

The reflection corner

Please use this page to reflect on last ten anxiety episodes.

Using free writing, look back, evaluate them, noting your "low points" (when you were stressed the most), noting situational, social or internal conditions surrounding the episodes. If you can, try to narrow down to what had prompted the episode.

Once you have concluded your anxiety reflection, try to recall a few happy moments within the same timeframe, if you can.

DATA COLLECTION: THE EXTENDED, AND AMENDED, QUESTIONNAIRE

As you have completed twenty anxiety record sheets during the last twenty anxiety episodes, you, more than likely, had begun to notice a pattern in your triggers, stimuli or situational factors that forewarn or trigger an episode.

So, in order to delve deeper, we will slightly shift gears with the next set of questionnaires. We will not only ask slightly different questions about each occurring episode, recording the experiences during the episode, as we have done it before, but we will begin to look into future, noting the outcome of an episode in more details, asking what we have learnt from that episode, reflecting, asking probing and analysing questions, which hopefully will give us an outline towards coping strategies and anxiety management techniques (about those we'll talk later).

Anxiety record sheet
Date

Situation What are you doing? Who are you with? What has happened?	Emotions and body sensations What do you feel?	Your thoughts What do you think will happen? What are your concerns, fears? Be honest.	Managing anxiety Record the outcome of the anxiety episode. What have you done? How have you coped?

Make it future proof.

Have you learnt anything from this episode?

Have you discovered new coping strategies? Have you implemented them?

LET'S GIVE GRATITUDE!

List three things that you've enjoyed today or which made you happy, no matter how small. We need to see that even in the anxiety-filled days we have something to be thankful for.

1.

2.

3.

Anxiety record sheet

Date

Situation What are you doing? Who are you with? What has happened?	Emotions and body sensations What do you feel?	Your thoughts What do you think will happen? What are your concerns, fears? Be honest.	Managing anxiety Record the outcome of the anxiety episode. What have you done? How have you coped?

Make it future proof.

Have you learnt anything from this episode?

Have you discovered new coping strategies? Have you implemented them?

LET'S GIVE GRATITUDE!

List three things that you've enjoyed today or which made you happy, no matter how small. We need to see that even in the anxiety-filled days we have something to be thankful for.

1.

2.

3.

Anxiety record sheet

Date

Situation What are you doing? Who are you with? What has happened?	Emotions and body sensations What do you feel?	Your thoughts What do you think will happen? What are your concerns, fears? Be honest.	Managing anxiety Record the outcome of the anxiety episode. What have you done? How have you coped?

Make it future proof.

Have you learnt anything from this episode?

Have you discovered new coping strategies? Have you implemented them?

LET'S GIVE GRATITUDE!

List three things that you've enjoyed today or which made you happy, no matter how small. We need to see that even in the anxiety-filled days we have something to be thankful for.

1.

2.

3.

Anxiety record sheet

Date

Situation What are you doing? Who are you with? What has happened?	Emotions and body sensations What do you feel?	Your thoughts What do you think will happen? What are your concerns, fears? Be honest.	Managing anxiety Record the outcome of the anxiety episode. What have you done? How have you coped?

Make it future proof.

Have you learnt anything from this episode?
Have you discovered new coping strategies? Have you implemented them?

LET'S GIVE GRATITUDE!

List three things that you've enjoyed today or which made you happy, no matter how small. We need to see that even in the anxiety-filled days we have something to be thankful for.

1.

2.

3.

Anxiety record sheet

Date

Situation What are you doing? Who are you with? What has happened?	Emotions and body sensations What do you feel?	Your thoughts What do you think will happen? What are your concerns, fears? Be honest.	Managing anxiety Record the outcome of the anxiety episode. What have you done? How have you coped?

Make it future proof.

Have you learnt anything from this episode?

Have you discovered new coping strategies? Have you implemented them?

LET'S GIVE GRATITUDE!

List three things that you've enjoyed today or which made you happy, no matter how small. We need to see that even in the anxiety-filled days we have something to be thankful for.

1.

2.

3.

Anxiety record sheet

Date

Situation What are you doing? Who are you with? What has happened?	Emotions and body sensations What do you feel?	Your thoughts What do you think will happen? What are your concerns, fears? Be honest.	Managing anxiety Record the outcome of the anxiety episode. What have you done? How have you coped?

Make it future proof.

Have you learnt anything from this episode?

Have you discovered new coping strategies? Have you implemented them?

LET'S GIVE GRATITUDE!

List three things that you've enjoyed today or which made you happy, no matter how small. We need to see that even in the anxiety-filled days we have something to be thankful for.

1.

2.

3.

Anxiety record sheet

Date

Situation What are you doing? Who are you with? What has happened?	Emotions and body sensations What do you feel?	Your thoughts What do you think will happen? What are your concerns, fears? Be honest.	Managing anxiety Record the outcome of the anxiety episode. What have you done? How have you coped?

Make it future proof.

Have you learnt anything from this episode?

Have you discovered new coping strategies? Have you implemented them?

LET'S GIVE GRATITUDE!

List three things that you've enjoyed today or which made you happy, no matter how small. We need to see that even in the anxiety-filled days we have something to be thankful for.

1.

2.

3.

Anxiety record sheet

Date

Situation What are you doing? Who are you with? What has happened?	Emotions and body sensations What do you feel?	Your thoughts What do you think will happen? What are your concerns, fears? Be honest.	Managing anxiety Record the outcome of the anxiety episode. What have you done? How have you coped?

Make it future proof.

Have you learnt anything from this episode?

Have you discovered new coping strategies? Have you implemented them?

LET'S GIVE GRATITUDE!

List three things that you've enjoyed today or which made you happy, no matter how small. We need to see that even in the anxiety-filled days we have something to be thankful for.

1.

2.

3.

Anxiety record sheet

Date

Situation What are you doing? Who are you with? What has happened?	Emotions and body sensations What do you feel?	Your thoughts What do you think will happen? What are your concerns, fears? Be honest.	Managing anxiety Record the outcome of the anxiety episode. What have you done? How have you coped?

Make it future proof.

Have you learnt anything from this episode?

Have you discovered new coping strategies? Have you implemented them?

LET'S GIVE GRATITUDE!

List three things that you've enjoyed today or which made you happy, no matter how small. We need to see that even in the anxiety-filled days we have something to be thankful for.

1.

2.

3.

Anxiety record sheet

Date

Situation What are you doing? Who are you with? What has happened?	Emotions and body sensations What do you feel?	Your thoughts What do you think will happen? What are your concerns, fears? Be honest.	Managing anxiety Record the outcome of the anxiety episode. What have you done? How have you coped?

Make it future proof.

Have you learnt anything from this episode?

Have you discovered new coping strategies? Have you implemented them?

LET'S GIVE GRATITUDE!

List three things that you've enjoyed today or which made you happy, no matter
how small. We need to see that even in the anxiety-filled days we have something to
be thankful for.

1.

2.

3.

The reflection corner

Please use this page to reflect on the last ten anxiety episodes.

Using free writing, look back, evaluate them, noting your "low points" (when you were stressed the most), whilst remembering to mention the "high", happy moments within the same timeframe.

Anxiety record sheet

Date

Situation What are you doing? Who are you with? What has happened?	Emotions and body sensations What do you feel?	Your thoughts What do you think will happen? What are your concerns, fears? Be honest.	Managing anxiety Record the outcome of the anxiety episode. What have you done? How have you coped?

Make it future proof.

Have you learnt anything from this episode?

Have you discovered new coping strategies? Have you implemented them?

LET'S GIVE GRATITUDE!

List three things that you've enjoyed today or which made you happy, no matter how small. We need to see that even in the anxiety-filled days we have something to be thankful for.

1.

2.

3.

Anxiety record sheet

Date

Situation What are you doing? Who are you with? What has happened?	Emotions and body sensations What do you feel?	Your thoughts What do you think will happen? What are your concerns, fears? Be honest.	Managing anxiety Record the outcome of the anxiety episode. What have you done? How have you coped?

Make it future proof.

Have you learnt anything from this episode?

Have you discovered new coping strategies? Have you implemented them?

LET'S GIVE GRATITUDE!

List three things that you've enjoyed today or which made you happy, no matter how small. We need to see that even in the anxiety-filled days we have something to be thankful for.

1.

2.

3.

Anxiety record sheet

Date

Situation What are you doing? Who are you with? What has happened?	Emotions and body sensations What do you feel?	Your thoughts What do you think will happen? What are your concerns, fears? Be honest.	Managing anxiety Record the outcome of the anxiety episode. What have you done? How have you coped?

Make it future proof.

Have you learnt anything from this episode?

Have you discovered new coping strategies? Have you implemented them?

LET'S GIVE GRATITUDE!

List three things that you've enjoyed today or which made you happy, no matter how small. We need to see that even in the anxiety-filled days we have something to be thankful for.

1.

2.

3.

Anxiety record sheet

Date

Situation	Emotions and body sensations	Your thoughts	Managing anxiety
What are you doing? Who are you with? What has happened?	What do you feel?	What do you think will happen? What are your concerns, fears? Be honest.	Record the outcome of the anxiety episode. What have you done? How have you coped?

Make it future proof.

Have you learnt anything from this episode?

Have you discovered new coping strategies? Have you implemented them?

LET'S GIVE GRATITUDE!

List three things that you've enjoyed today or which made you happy, no matter how small. We need to see that even in the anxiety-filled days we have something to be thankful for.

1.

2.

3.

Anxiety record sheet

Date

Situation What are you doing? Who are you with? What has happened?	Emotions and body sensations What do you feel?	Your thoughts What do you think will happen? What are your concerns, fears? Be honest.	Managing anxiety Record the outcome of the anxiety episode. What have you done? How have you coped?

Make it future proof.

Have you learnt anything from this episode?

Have you discovered new coping strategies? Have you implemented them?

LET'S GIVE GRATITUDE!

List three things that you've enjoyed today or which made you happy, no matter how small. We need to see that even in the anxiety-filled days we have something to be thankful for.

1.

2.

3.

Anxiety record sheet

Date

Situation What are you doing? Who are you with? What has happened?	Emotions and body sensations What do you feel?	Your thoughts What do you think will happen? What are your concerns, fears? Be honest.	Managing anxiety Record the outcome of the anxiety episode. What have you done? How have you coped?

Make it future proof.

Have you learnt anything from this episode?

Have you discovered new coping strategies? Have you implemented them?

LET'S GIVE GRATITUDE!

List three things that you've enjoyed today or which made you happy, no matter how small. We need to see that even in the anxiety-filled days we have something to be thankful for.

1.

2.

3.

Anxiety record sheet

Date

Situation What are you doing? Who are you with? What has happened?	Emotions and body sensations What do you feel?	Your thoughts What do you think will happen? What are your concerns, fears? Be honest.	Managing anxiety Record the outcome of the anxiety episode. What have you done? How have you coped?

Make it future proof.

Have you learnt anything from this episode?

Have you discovered new coping strategies? Have you implemented them?

LET'S GIVE GRATITUDE!

List three things that you've enjoyed today or which made you happy, no matter how small. We need to see that even in the anxiety-filled days we have something to be thankful for.

1.

2.

3.

Anxiety record sheet

Date

Situation	Emotions and body sensations	Your thoughts	Managing anxiety
What are you doing? Who are you with? What has happened?	What do you feel?	What do you think will happen? What are your concerns, fears? Be honest.	Record the outcome of the anxiety episode. What have you done? How have you coped?

Make it future proof.

Have you learnt anything from this episode?

Have you discovered new coping strategies? Have you implemented them?

LET'S GIVE GRATITUDE!

List three things that you've enjoyed today or which made you happy, no matter how small. We need to see that even in the anxiety-filled days we have something to be thankful for.

1.

2.

3.

Anxiety record sheet

Date

Situation What are you doing? Who are you with? What has happened?	Emotions and body sensations What do you feel?	Your thoughts What do you think will happen? What are your concerns, fears? Be honest.	Managing anxiety Record the outcome of the anxiety episode. What have you done? How have you coped?

Make it future proof.

Have you learnt anything from this episode?

Have you discovered new coping strategies? Have you implemented them?

LET'S GIVE GRATITUDE!

List three things that you've enjoyed today or which made you happy, no matter how small. We need to see that even in the anxiety-filled days we have something to be thankful for.

1.

2.

3.

Anxiety record sheet

Date

Situation What are you doing? Who are you with? What has happened?	Emotions and body sensations What do you feel?	Your thoughts What do you think will happen? What are your concerns, fears? Be honest.	Managing anxiety Record the outcome of the anxiety episode. What have you done? How have you coped?

Make it future proof.

Have you learnt anything from this episode?

Have you discovered new coping strategies? Have you implemented them?

LET'S GIVE GRATITUDE!

List three things that you've enjoyed today or which made you happy, no matter how small. We need to see that even in the anxiety-filled days we have something to be thankful for.

1.

2.

3.

The reflection corner

Please use this page to reflect on the last ten episodes.

Using free writing, look back, evaluate them, noting your "low points" (when you were stressed the most), whilst remembering to mention the "high", happy moments within the same timeframe.

PART 4
ANALYSIS

TRIGGERS

Being able to assess anxiety cues and triggers in a reliable way is essential for establishing a diagnosis, for developing an appropriate treatment plan, and for measuring treatment outcome (Antony and Rowa, "Evidence-Based Assessment of Anxiety Disorders in Adults", Psychological Assessment).

And for that purpose, diaries are often implemented. They are used to record and then assess situational cues and triggers, so that on the basis of the gathered data, the management plan can be developed, and then implemented. Therefore, using the "Reflection model" and gathered data, please compile a personal list of triggers below. Take your time. Be honest with yourself. Reflect, but with kindness to yourself in mind.

My anxiety triggers

This page is for recording your anxiety triggers. Over the course of time, with the help of your anxiety records, you can identify situations in which your anxieties occur more often. Look for a pattern. Does your anxiety occur at the same time of day, maybe in the same location or situation, or when you around the same people? Could it be triggered by a sight, smell or sound? And if so, what associations are there?

1.

2.

3.

4.

5.

6.

7.

8.

Please use the next page if you need to list more triggers. And remember, this list with change over time: some triggers might dissipate with the help of exposure therapy, whilst some new triggers might find their way onto this list.

My anxiety triggers
(If required, continue on this page)

MY TRIGGERS

For better and in depth understanding of the triggers that affecting your anxiety, let's do another exercise: organize your earlier compiled list of triggers from the most tolerable triggers, the ones you could overcome with ease or with very little internal work, to the least tolerable triggers, the ones which you would struggle or unable to overcome.

Please list the most tolerable triggers at the bottom of the table, moderately tolerable triggers in the middle, and least tolerable triggers at the top of the table. The benefit of this exercise is that it would provide a clear and visual guide to your anxieties and another way in understanding your triggers. It would give you another glimpse into your anxiety – how it's affecting you, and what it is affected by.

The least tolerable triggers	
Moderately tolerable triggers	
The most tolerable triggers	

The reflection "station"

Let's pause for a moment and take stock, and look back.

Looking through your anxiety journal, identify the most common situations in which you experienced anxiety.

Can you avoid these situations? Are these situations instrumental in the quality of your life or can you cut them out of your life without losing quality of life? Are they social or situational? Are they prompted by people or locations? Can you do anything to minimise the spike of anxiety in these situations?

Situation	Can you avoid it? Should you?	What can you do to minimise your anxiety related to this situation?

LET'S TALK AVOIDANCE

In this chapter we will discuss **avoidance**.

On the previous page, you have compiled a list of situations, which makes you uncomfortable, situations, which you believe are responsible for anxiety episodes, situations that you'll try to avoid if you're given a chance.

When it comes to anxiety, many of us are choosing to implement **avoidance** as an emotion-regulating strategy. Basically, when we know that something is threatening us, instead of confronting the issue and work through it, to "push through", to develop sustainable coping mechanisms, we choose to avoid the threat and leave the dangerous situation altogether, in some instances, refusing to enter certain social situations for fear to have a panic or anxiety attack.

Avoidance is the first, instinctive reaction to threat. It is prompted by the centuries-long cultivated self-preservation, and although, there's something to be said for implementing that technique in dealing with dangers, avoidance should not be used for repeat, persistent environmental threats.

Avoidance comes on the back of the identified triggers: we understand what triggers us, and then we avoid those situations (places, people) in a bid to eliminate a trigger, thus to prevent an episode.

If we've lived with the condition long enough, we know in which situations anxiety comes, or what triggers could've prompted anxiety.

Indeed, the vigilance-avoidance hypothesis describes avoidance as "the strategic directing of attention away from threat... a definition that may fit better with the concept of distraction..."

The research carried out by Price demonstrated that within the vigilance-avoidance model, anxious individuals, relative to non-anxious individuals, orient quicker to threatening stimuli and then later avoid the said stimuli. That is, initial orienting to threat may be followed by subsequent avoidance of the threatening stimuli; a socially anxious individual have their attention captured by threat cues, and then direct the attention away from those cues in order to reduce their subjective discomfort (Price et al, "Vigilance in the laboratory predicts avoidance in the real world: A dimensional analysis of neural, behavioural, and ecological momentary data in anxious youth", Developmental Cognitive Neuroscience).

In the context of anxiety, the benefits of avoidance are very short lived.

It's well documented that as sufferers, we don't allow ourselves to develop managing mechanisms to common, or manageable, stimuli or situations. Locking ourselves away, we don't give ourselves chance to grow, to become stronger and more resilient, although, it is well-known that repeated exposure to stimuli will cause a decrease in reaction to the said stimuli.

Avoidance is very common. The avoidance of situations or objects that can trigger us is common across the spectrum of anxiety disorders. It's usually the first and the most common way in managing uncomfortable situations. For example, avoidance of internal experiences, referred to by specialists as experiential avoidance, is also a common feature of anxiety disorders. Therefore, individuals with PTSD try to avoid experiencing traumatic memories, and individuals with OCD may suppress obsessions with aggressive, religious, or sexual content.

But the way forward does not lies in avoidance. In clinical settings, treatment of anxiety disorders always includes measured exposure to feared objects, situations, thoughts, and sensations.

The way forward is always the way through.

As much as this might sound scary, and unpleasant, this is arguably the most reliable way to treat anxieties, and to provide long-term relief.

But in order to compile a personalised anxiety treatment plan, evidence and pattern of personal ***situational avoidance*** should be gathered. This way of managing anxiety manifestations has been proven to address avoidance behaviour, and controlled and limited exposure has been proven to improve anxiety, its triggers, resulting in milder symptoms and then, ***desensitising.***

The exposure is the primary mechanism of action when dealing with anxieties, therefore, amplifying exposure techniques may be beneficial, enhancing and furthering the successful outcomes.

And how could we measure the results of the controlled exposure? The reductions in avoidance are usually a good indicator of improvement.

Earlier in the book, we have recorded triggers. Then, we reflected on situations we find difficult, honestly listing situations which we try to avoid, knowing from experience that those situations inevitably will lead to an anxiety episode.

Now, we will take a step further in managing our anxieties: we will compile a list of situations, or places, that we try to avoid. We will arrange those avoidance situations from the least tolerable to mildly uncomfortable.

This list "Avoidance Hierarchy" will help us to understand what are those personal situations, and when we will begin working on controlled and measured exposure, we will begin with mildly uncomfortable situations, then progressing to difficult situations, eventually, over time, culminating with exposure to personally intolerable situations.

The aim is to re-learn responses to those situations. We need to demonstrate to our brain and the nervous system that we can manage those situations: step by step, slowly, but always progressing forward.

AVOIDANCE HIERARCHY

Situation Anxiety (0-100%)
Let's construct a pyramid of places or situations that you try to avoid. At the top of the pyramid put those situations which make you most anxious. At the bottom, put the places or situations that you tend to avoid, but which don't bother you as much. In the middle of the pyramid put ones that are 'in-between'. Give each entry a rating from 0-100% according to how anxious you would feel if you had to be in that situation. Overcome your anxiety by approaching these situations, starting from the bottom of the pyramid, with the least troublesome situations, slowly progressing to the top. The aim of this exercise is not the speed, but consistency – take your time, but move forward!

(CONTINUE ON THIS PAGE)

PART 5
FUTURE-PROOF YOURSELF

EXPOSURE

"What doesn't kill you makes you stronger."

I already imagine the mass eye-roll at this phrase. But before you close this book and hurl it across the room, please read a bit further, and I will explain it. I hope I'd be able to demonstrate to you, and convince you, how to go about the measured exposure – how to create, and then manage it, and what benefits it holds for the management of anxieties and their symptoms.

The above old saying is apt when it comes to managing anxieties. Overtime, this phrase has been adopted into developing long-term management techniques, which were devised to improve anxiety's manifestations.

There's a scientific name for that saying: hormesis, which is basically a biological phenomenon where a positive effect results from exposure to low doses of something that is otherwise negative in higher doses.

There have been a number published researches showing that low-dose controlled stressors such as oxygen restriction, intermittent fasting or cold water exposure are all could be used for beneficial outcome to stimulate the hormetic response.

Some researches had shown that cold water exposure helps to decrease cortisol levels and increase the levels of the feel-good neurotransmitter serotonin. The adrenaline rush you get from immersing yourself in cold water creates a rush of norepinephrine, which helps to increase energy, focus, and performance outcomes. And although, that's not the main point of our discussion, it's an interesting development in understanding our brain activity, which some of you might choose to try and utilise at some point.

Hormones and neurotransmitters kick into gear during these controlled exposures, leading to an increase in physiological and mental resilience. It's one of the wheels of evolution.

There are many theories, which are then, in turn, utilised in CBT practice that exposure therapy for anxiety disorders is likely to lead to a future individual's engagement in similar situations, thus reducing anxiety over time. For example, using relaxation as a learned coping response to approach situations increases self-efficacy and a sense of performance accomplishment, which in turn decreases negative, fused reactions related to anxiety in these situations.

Engaging in previously avoided, potentially anxiety provoking situations allows us to learn new behaviour, in turn changing our behaviour/response over time.

Exposure-based treatments, which are effective in reducing fear and anxiety in a variety of anxiety disorders has been shown to promote new learning when the individual approaches the feared stimulus, yet the feared outcome does not occur.

Exposure enhances acceptance by demonstrating that it is possible to engage in varied situations while experiencing anxiety.

Applied together, measured exposure combined with relaxation strategies can teach us how to confront and manage previously uncomfortable and damaging situations.

CONTROLLED EXPOSURE

In his research, Hilderbrandt had clearly demonstrated that exposure and habituation to triggers are the primary mechanism of change. This was evident when over time his participants had experienced decreased anxiety in response to anxious stimuli and triggers, and to mandatory elimination of their avoidance behaviours (Hilderbrandt et al, "Anxiety in Anorexia Nervosa and its Management UsingFamily-Based Treatment", European Disorders Review).

Basically, the more often they were exposed to anxious stimuli, the less they were worried by them.

Habituation is decrease in response to a stimulus after repeated presentations, and that's exactly what we want to achieve through the controlled exposure.

When one had achieved a greater understanding of his/her pattern in the stimuli, he/she then can work on responses: at first, developing an avoidance mechanism, as the way to improve immediate response to condition, or as a short term solution, and then beginning to work on introducing limited and controlled exposure in order to achieve de-sensitization, or habituation.

With limited and controlled exposure, we give ourselves a chance to "dip a toe" into the frightening waters of anxious situations, whilst, at the same time, being in control and able to withdraw at a moment notice should the situation become too unbearable.

But the intensity of the exposure must progressively increase over time.

Once the triggers were identified, the situations during which anxiety was experienced **must be repeated**, time and time again, thus providing us with the desensitisation to that particular trigger.

So, the first step in better anxiety management is understanding your anxiety, and the answer to that is data collection that we have done earlier.

Then, it's down to analysing the triggers, arranging them, while understanding the discomfort they cause.

And finally: implement the gradual (controlled) exposure to those triggers – starting with the least uncomfortable trigger, slowly progressing up the pyramid.

TYPES OF EXPOSURE

There is more than one type of exposure utilised in anxiety management during CBT sessions, but below are notable few.

- ***Imaginal Exposure***. In this type of exposure, a person in therapy is asked to mentally confront the fear or situation by picturing it in his/her mind. For example, a person with agoraphobia, a fear of crowded places, might imagine standing in a crowded area, stadium, shopping centre etc, or a person who is afraid of heights might imagine standing on top of a cliff. Often a visual aid is utilised with this exposure, for example photo or video images to encourage the immersiveness.

- ***In-Vivo Exposure***. When using this type of exposure, a person is exposed to real-life objects and scenarios. For example, a person with a fear of flying might go to the airport and watch a plane take off. With this situational exposure, it is beneficial to engage with it either with a help of a practitioner, or with a support of a friend.

- ***Virtual Reality Exposure***: This type of exposure combines elements of both imaginal and in vivo exposure so that a person is placed in situations that appear real but are actually fabricated. For example, someone who has a fear of heights—acrophobia—might participate in a virtual simulation of climbing down a fire escape.

EXPOSURE THERAPY TECHNIQUES

Below are some of the Exposure Therapy Techniques that CBT researchers and practitioners have developed over the last decades.

The exercises that are proposed in this book are building on these techniques, while simplifying the process.

Often the below techniques are supplemented with the cognitive re-structuring technique, and although, it is highly beneficial while working with phobias, we won't cover the cognitive re-structuring here, as it is highly personalised.

- **Systematic Desensitization**: This technique incorporates relaxation training, the development of an anxiety hierarchy (which we have done earlier), and gradual exposure to the feared item or situation. The aim of this practice is, with the help of the learned relaxation techniques, to offset anxiety-induced situations, starting with the least frightening situation.

- **Graded Exposure**: This technique is similar to systematic desensitization, but does not integrate the use of relaxation techniques.

- **Flooding**: In this technique, exposure can be in vivo or imaginal. A person is intensely exposed to anxiety-evoking events for a prolonged period of time. Flooding is usually done until the anxiety is significantly diminished.

- **Prolonged Exposure (PE)**: Proven effective with trauma-related issues, this technique is similar to flooding but also incorporates psycho-education and cognitive processing.

- **Exposure and Response Prevention (ERP)**: An effective technique for people experiencing obsessions and compulsions, ERP works to weaken the link between obsessions and compulsions. Therapists provoke a person's obsessions and then ask that person not to engage in their behavioural rituals or compulsions.

EXPOSURE EXERCISE (1)

Sit down in a quiet and empty room.

Get a clock or a timer.

Make sure that your phone is turned off.

Relax.

Begin with meditation or a calming technique of your choosing. Note the time on the clock.

Close your eyes.

Then, using an "Imaginal Exposure" technique, imagine that you are walking down the familiar road (countryside, woods, beach), slowly approaching the situation that causes you anxiety (a crowded place, or a place where dog sits, or a slow and gentle climb up the hill etc).

You're progressing towards your anxiety, and you know it.

Your pulse quickens, but you don't turn away. You don't stop, and you don't open your eyes.

You're progressing towards your anxiety, closer and closer.

Do this exercise regularly, until you don't feel uncomfortable or scared imagining yourself amidst your anxiety-inducing situation (an exam room, a top of a cliff, confronting your boss, a neighbour's dog etc). The key is detailed and steady progression.

Record below how many minutes you've managed inside your anxiety-inducing situation. The goal is to spend as much time, as comfortably possible inside you anxiety-inducing situation, until you feel in control and calm in that situation.

CONTINUE RECORDING OUTCOME OF IMAGINAL EXPOSURE EXERSICES HERE

EXPOSURE EXERCISE (2)

Building on "Imaginal Exposure", this "Real life exposure" techniques used on the back of the imaginal exposure exercises, or separately, when you feel that you can take practiced techniques of relaxation and anxiety management into the real world.

Real life exposure. Unlike with "Imaginal Exposure" this exposure exercise should take place not in our mind, but in the real world.

Pick one of the least stressful situations, from your "Avoidance hierarchy" pyramid that you have assembled in Part 4. It would be beneficial if you've already worked with this anxiety-induced situation during your imaginal exposure. Or choose one of the least damaging triggers that prompts your anxiety (that list should be available for you in the same place -Part 4 – remember? I did promise you that all data gathering and the arranging of stressful situations and triggering stimuli will come in handy later in the book!)

Now, immerse yourself in that situation.

Take yourself into that situation. Take a friend along, if you need a moral help.

But remember: start with the least avoidant situations and least threatening triggers!

For example: If you're afraid of talking to strangers, go to a shop and start a conversation with a cashier; if you're afraid of dogs, take a look at puppies in the store window; if you're afraid of flying – go to the airport, and so on.

Record on this page a chosen trigger, steps taken toward the exposure, and outcome.

And remember: You don't need to make a large step, as even a small step towards confronting your anxious situation is already a break through.

CONTINUE RECORDING THE REAL LIFE EXPOSURE EXERCISES HERE

PART 6
RESULTS & OUTCOMES

EVALUATION

Hopefully you have been recording during the course of this book: recording your triggers, while analysing them, then raking them from the worst to least damaging triggers; recording your avoidance patterns in the avoidance hierarchy; recording your meditation and relaxation techniques, the length of them too; recording your exercises – what triggers you've worked with, for how long, what technique you've used.

If you have recorded all of that, you now have a vast amount of data to work with – not only in understanding your triggers, but in the work you've carried out.

In this chapter, we'll look at how far you have come. Here we evaluate and compare.

Before and after, so to speak.

And for that, below, you have two tables to collate.

Look back at the list of recorded triggers in the Part 4. Feel free to update that list of triggers and to add more, new ones, if you wish – as, at the end of the day, you have done a lot of hard work in self-discovery and self-understanding, so there are, understandably, might be new discoveries (pleasant or otherwise).

Now record the same triggers from the table in the Part 4 in the table below, placing them in the order of their anxiety-inducing damage to you.

Now, looking at the two tables side by side, note if there are any triggers that had moved within the table, becoming less intolerable, milder.

Of course we want to see an improvement in regards to triggers' position within the table, but we need to be honest with ourselves first and foremost. We need to understand what is working, and what is not, if we want to develop a long-term management techniques.

If you have noted an improvement even in one of the triggers – it's already a huge win! Be proud of yourself and the work you have done.

But above all, note the technique or exercise you've used with that particular trigger, as this might be the answer for your personal long-term anxiety management.

LIST OF PERSONAL TRIGGERS (ARRANGED IN ORDER OF ANXIETY-INDUCING SEVERITY) – UPDATED AFTER THE CARRIED OUT WORK.	
The least tolerable triggers AFTER CARRIED OUT WORK	
Moderately tolerable triggers AFTER CARRIED OUT WORK	
The most tolerable triggers AFTER CARRIED OUT WORK	

PERSONAL TRIGGERS – POST "CARRIED-OUT WORK"			
A TRIGGER	IT'S POSITION ON THE LIST OF TRIGGERS BEFORE THE WORK & EXERCISES	THE WORK CARRIED OUT: EXERCISE TECHNIQUES USED, MEDITATION, RELAXATION ETC	THE TRIGGER'S POSITION ON THE PERSONAL LIST OF TRIGGERS AFTEER THE CARRIED-OUT WORK

THE POWER OF POSITIVE THINKING

There's a term in CBT: **Expectancy violation**. It's when we expect one thing to happen, but something completely different happens instead. This is a very powerful tool to bend and mould our prerequisite thinking. When working with anxieties, it has been known to empirically demonstrate to us that our fears were unfounded, that we were wrong in our pre-leant knowledge, in our situational avoidance. From inhibitory learning perspective, expectancy violation is helpful because it promotes stronger learning.

So, in order to continue the evaluation, and to future-proof ourselves, here's another exercise for you.

During the course of the book, we have discussed how the earlier learnt life lessons affect our future decision-making, how one negative outcome of an episode could prevent us from trying to do it again: we've learnt that "X situation = danger", and we operate on that knowledge. Yes, I'm talking about our developed avoidance patterns and strategies, which we have discussed earlier.

So, in order to enjoy life to the full and to be open for new experiences, try to look back through your log of the recorded episodes, and find that negative thought pattern – for example, thoughts that came to your mind while you were experiencing an anxiety attack).

Then, after looking back at the outcome of a situation, record in the table below if your fears have been fulfilled.

The goal here is to find that moment, or an episode, of expectancy violation. Finding and recording those incidents will help you to analyse you behaviour pattern, over time, negating the developed avoidance strategies – expectancy violation is very powerful tool!

Or, alternatively, try to turn that negative and damaging thought into a positive one. For example: *I will fail at this test.* Did you get a 'fail'? *I only can do my best in this test.*

EXPECTANCY VIOLATION		
Negative thought	**Was the thought fulfilled?**	**Positive thought**

CONTINUE RECORDING HERE

THE FUTURE IS BRIGHT!

The future is bright!

Introspection is the informal reflection process, examining one's internal thoughts and feelings and reflecting on what they mean. It helps you to stay on the right path of self-reflection, asking "what" questions rather than "why" questions. "Why" questions can highlight our limitations and stir up negative emotions, while "what" questions help keep us curious and positive about the future (Eurich, 2017).

With this important point in mind, let's move on to the final questions and thoughts to evaluate the course of this book on your anxiety management.

With broader strokes, look back on the experience.

Have you learnt anything about your anxieties over the course of this book?

Have you discovered new management techniques?

Have you implemented any?

Which of them worked?

How do you feel about your anxieties now?

Has the number of your overall (daily, weekly, monthly) anxiety episodes decreased?

No matter how small your victory seems at this time, record it all below.

MY ANXIETY AND ME

Drawing, doodling or using free writing technique, this is your space to express your relationship with your anxiety now.

Do you understand it better? Is it as dark and big as it was before? Do you know your triggers now? How can this knowledge empower you? Can you minimise the severity of your anxiety attacks?

Reflect on this book and on the work you have done, and record it here.

Notes